ANCHORLESS

JOLIE P. HOANG

 FriesenPress

Suite 300 - 990 Fort St
Victoria, BC, V8V 3K2
Canada

www.friesenpress.com

ISBN
978-1-5255-5910-5 (Hardcover)
978-1-5255-5911-2 (Paperback)
978-1-5255-5912-9 (eBook)

1. BIOGRAPHY & AUTOBIOGRAPHY, PERSONAL MEMOIRS

Distributed to the trade by The Ingram Book Company

For my father, Hoàng Trọng Phụ, with love and respect

For my dearest sister: Hoàng Thị Lan Phương

It took me thirty years to accept our fates

&

For my mother, Võ Thị Sĩ, with love and admiration

For your many years of enduring love and loneliness

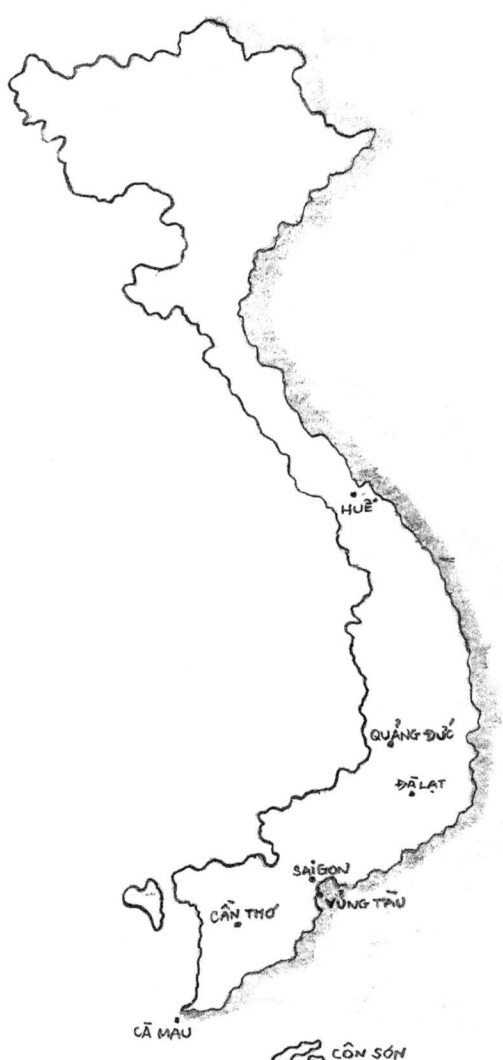

HUẾ

QUẢNG ĐỨC

ĐÀ LẠT

SÀI GÒN
CẦN THƠ
VŨNG TÀU

CÀ MAU

CÔN SƠN

INTRODUCTION

IF I HAD A CHANCE TO CHANGE THE past, I would want to go back to the time when I escaped from Vietnam in May 1983. I would want my father, my mother, and my three younger siblings to escape altogether with us, instead of me and my four brothers, two sisters, and a sister-in-law first escaping Vietnam on our own.

June 15, 2015 would be Lan Phương's birthday. She was my youngest sister. This day also marked exactly thirty years since her death, and my father's death. She died on her birthday. Vietnamese peoples rarely celebrated birthdays back then. Instead of nine birthday candles on her cake, memorial incenses needed to be lighted. My youngest sister does not have a grave. She died in the ocean; her body was never recovered.

We buried our father for the last time on April 25, 2015, in California. I attended this funeral this time, unlike back in 1985, when I was here in Canada hearing the sad news. For years, I did not have a clear idea of how to accept his death. Not until that day, his final funeral, when his cremated ashes were in America, and I held his remains for the last time before he was buried. I realized that, over the years, since I had never attended his funeral, I was in denial about his death. I could never accept it.

This year, on his death anniversary, I did not hold a memorial. I felt extremely sad. It bothered me as to why I did not want to do it. Over the years, I'd held a memorial conscientiously each year. Now, my father had finally fulfilled his wish to reunite with his children in America. The fact that only his ashes arrived, and had been buried in foreign soil, sadly struck me. The reality sunk in. My father was, in fact, gone.

Dearest Father and Sister,
It took me thirty years to be able to accept our fates.
This book is written for you, for many unsaid words,
for many untold stories, for a lifetime of lost times,
for my imagination to fulfill all that has been lost.

Dearest Father,
I had to be parted from you, and could only live
with you for a short seventeen years. Instead of our
lifetime together, fate cruelly cut it short.

Dearest Sister,
Instead of celebrating your birthday together every
year, I have to light incense to remember your death.

ESCAPE FROM VIETNAM

VƯỢT BIÊN

1

1985
MY DEATH

I DIED WHEN I WAS SIXTY YEARS OLD. I was a husband, and a father of ten living children. My death was not natural. I died with my youngest daughter, who was nine years old at the time. I died when I attempted to reunite with my six older children, who were living oceans apart from me. My six older children are: First son, Second daughter, Second son, Third son, Third daughter, and Fourth son. I will not name them here. They were in Canada, halfway around the earth. I died while escaping Vietnam on a small boat, with my wife and my three younger children, and with the hope of reuniting the family. I died in the Pacific Ocean in Vietnam, while trying to shorten the distance between us all.

When I died, my soul flew and arrived at the door of Heaven. I begged God to please allow me to not yet enter Heaven. Let me live as a ghost. Let the dead stay with the living. Let my soul not rest and stay with my children. God told me that it was my time in the book of Heaven. A dead person dared not defy his fate. He or she dared not go against what was written in the book of Heaven. I cried, but a soul could not shed any tears. I felt pain, but I could not express the suffering.

God demanded me to hurry and step through the door before it closed upon me.

"Why would you want more suffering?" God asked me firmly. "While in death, you are free of the living. In Heaven, you are at eternal peace. Give me a good reason to let you live as a ghost."

"When I died," I told God, "I could still hear my children's anguished cries, and then I could hear their silent cries. I hear the tears in their hearts. I will do anything for you, God. Please, I beg you to let my soul not rest, but live on as a ghost."

God was stirred by also hearing the anguished cries of the living: of my eight surviving children, my dead children, my wife, my mother, my dead father, my grandchildren, my brothers, my sisters, and my friends.

Before granting my wish, God gave me a lecture:

"Living as a ghost, you still have memories of your past. You want to say your thoughts, but you cannot talk. You want to forget, but you still remember. You want to feel, but you cannot touch. You want to cry, but tears are not shed. You are present only to yourself. You are invisible to the living."

I found myself growing angry, as God asked, "Is my Heaven meaningless to you? Heaven is created for those who have done their time on earth. It is time for your tired soul to rest. Death comes to you when your physical being can no longer endure any more pain. It is a relief. It is quite strange to hear such a request. Why would you want to prolong your agony?"

Then, suddenly, God stopped lecturing and listened. God heard the cries. God realized that, in death, I was still suffering. God concluded that I needed time to learn the true meaning of death. God granted my wish, and released my soul.

"You are now living between life and death. What can you do for your children with your helpless soul? Perhaps, you want to find the answers on your own."

2

CÔN SƠN ISLAND, VIETNAM
A PRISON
MY FIRST FUNERAL

I RUSHED TO THE PLACE WHERE I DIED. It was Côn Sơn Island, located near where the boat sank. I found my body buried without a coffin, in a shallow grave surrounded by stones. The plastic bag, which should have contained my dead body, had been carefully rolled, and tucked under my feet. Underneath the ground, big and small stones also surrounded my lifeless body. Someone purposely buried me in this way and marked my grave. I realized that it had been done with a goal of finding my body later. It would be faster for the body to be decomposed. It would also be easy to exhume at a later time. It was a terribly sad sight, but it was a good thing. I would not want my body to be buried on a strange island anyway. A marked grave meant there had to be an intention to move my body later. I came to realize that this was my first funeral, the poorest and the saddest one. I thought of my wife and my three young children, who were with me in the attempt to escape, and perhaps, had survived.

I wandered on the island. I went to the prison site where they imprisoned those who tried to escape from their own country. I found my wife and my two young sons, who were fourteen and twelve at the time. I almost could not recognize them. They were skinny and full of grief. Where was my youngest daughter? She was not with them. I asked my wife where our youngest daughter was. I screamed and realized that no one could hear me. They were lying on a dirty mat, in a large, filthy prison cell with many other prisoners. I recognized some of them. They were my fellow escapees. My wife was weeping silently. My young sons were hungry. I could feel the immense sorrow in their hearts. I felt a sharp pain in my own. I crumbled to the ground, but the pain did not go away. I had no tears to wash away the agony. I leapt over to them. I tried to caress and to hug them, but they did not respond to me. I was invisible to them. God had warned me. I was a miserable ghost and a helpless soul.

3

MY YOUNGEST DAUGHTER HOÀNG THỊ LAN PHƯƠNG

I TRIED TO WHISPER INTO MY WIFE'S EARS, hoping she could hear me asking where our youngest daughter was. Suddenly, I heard someone call me:

"Father, is that you?"

I recognized the familiar voice of my youngest child. I called her name. She appeared. I could see her: my beloved daughter. I hugged her tenderly. She responded to me. She felt me. We felt each other. Then I realized that she was just like me: a ghost! She embraced me with her lost soul. A confused soul could not rise to heaven. She said that she was waiting for me, like she always did. I heard her. We could see each other's hollow eyes, which were unable to shed tears. Together, father and daughter grieved in deep sorrow. Together, as ghosts, we understood each other.

"Father, where were you? What happened to us, Dad?" asked my daughter. Her voice trembled.

I held her tiny hands. Together, we leapt our souls to the

ocean, to the spot where the boat sank. We went under the seawater and found my daughter's body, which was trapped in the boat along with other dead bodies. We heard and saw other anguished ghosts. We avoided them, found a piece of floating debris, and sat on it. The sky was dark purple. The waves were strong, as if they were trying to swallow the lost souls. However, our souls were so light, weightless ... floating along with the angry waves.

"Why is my body down there, Dad?" my daughter asked me, sadly.

I was with her in sadness. "Dearest daughter, we both died from drowning. Somehow, my body is buried on land, and yours is still trapped with the boat."

4

1981
THE FIRST ESCAPE
A POSTCARD FROM GERMANY

VIETNAM WAS IN TURMOIL. THE AFTEREFFECTS OF THE war put most families into a tremendously hard time. I lost my business and my wealth to the communist government. I was able to bribe the communist officials to keep my home and my family in the city of Đà Lạt. My family was on the list to be sent to an economist-reformed land. Uncertainty was constantly in my mind. I did not know what to do for the future of my ten children. We lived day by day, with enough food on the table, but not knowing what the communist government would do to our family status. The economist-reform policy could be imposed on my family at any time. I lived in constant worry and fear. I could get by with the innocence of my children, the obedience and the understanding that they gave me. Most important of all, it was their daily laughter that kept me going.

One day, I came home from an odd job and my second

son showed me a postcard that he had received from his friend. The postcard was sent to my son from Germany. Many families had tried to escape the country by boat. His family was among them. My second son mentioned that, one day, his friend had just stopped coming to school. No one asked about him. No one questioned or alerted the school officials. In the back of everyone's mind, we all knew that the family had escaped. After escaping, he settled in Germany. I borrowed the postcard from my second son and kept looking at it. I held on to it and stayed up that entire night. The freedom, the opportunities of life for this young man who sent this postcard, were endless. It could happen to my children too. I decided to make it happen. The postcard began the new and even more dangerous phase of my family life.

I had hidden gold ingots. The communist government could not take everything from me. My gold and my mind were the most powerful tools in going ahead with the plan. The postcard from Germany was my catalyst. I used some of my gold to arrange the first escape for my three oldest sons. I gave an amount of gold to a human smuggler, since they only accepted gold to carry out the deal. The title of human smuggler was not very attractive, but it was the right term. The human smugglers were the only ones who could arrange for the escape.

The years from 1978 to roughly 1988 were called the decade of the Vietnamese Boat People. The Vietnamese communist government turned a blind eye to let these escapes happen. It was an agenda to expose the hidden gold and diamonds from the people—people like me, from whom obvious wealth, such as houses, cars, and businesses had been immediately confiscated after the North Vietnamese communists took over South Vietnam in 1975.

The communist government would try anything to get their hands on people's secret-stack-away wealth. The communist officials would accept the hefty amount of gold or diamonds to loosen the coastguards along stretches of the Pacific Ocean. Most of the fishing ports were like an open sea. The strategy was to pave the way for the people with the gold and diamonds to escape. The escapees then would have to expose their hidden wealth. The smugglers who arranged such a trip would get a huge share of the gold and the diamonds as well.

My three sons were told to travel to Cần Thơ. They were secretly brought to a spot near a fishing port. They were gathered with some other escapees. Just as they were to run to a boat, they heard a scream, "Policeman! Policeman! Run! Run! Run fast for your life! Or you will be captured and put in prison!" The scream seemed to come from nowhere.

My three sons ran as fast as they could. They hid at a nearby supermarket until dark. They found their way back home by bus the very next day. The whole thing had been a setup. The smugglers disappeared. My gold ingots were gone. I could not tell anyone. I could not report the human smugglers whose scheme was to deceive me and steal my gold. If I revealed their scheme, I could be arrested too. I felt so stupid and anguished. I figured out that there had been no boat to escape in, and no policemen waiting to catch the escapees.

The whole escape arrangement had been a scam—a scam

that took advantage of human vulnerability in this tumultuous time. It was a scam that struck the human desire for freedom and brought that desire to a tragic halt. It was the wicked scam. It was also the best way to openly steal the people's wealth. I slowly comforted my own disappointment. At least my three sons had come back alive. The scammer could have arranged a non-functional boat and brought the escapees a short distance into the rough sea. Their lives could have been lost before they could even get caught and put in prison.

5

1982
I DECIDED TO BUILD AN ESCAPE BOAT!

I LEARNED MY BITTER AND UNFAIR LESSON IN desolation. I could not let go of the thought of arranging for my family to escape Vietnam. The postcard from Germany remained in my mind. I asked my son if I could keep it in the pocket of my jacket. It was a reminder to maintain my courage. It was also my amulet to soothe my conscience. I decided to leave my family behind in Đà Lạt. With a few gold ingots left, I left my parental responsibilities to my wife.

Đà Lạt was a plateau situated 1,500 metres above sea level. The atmospheric pressure created fogs, rains, and little sunshine. It was raining very hard on the day I left. Water soaked through my thin raincoat. My children thought I'd just left for another odd job. The night before I left, I could not sleep. I stood beside my children's beds. They had to share the beds. All the brothers were in two beds in the same bedroom. All the sisters were in another. I watched

15

them sleep for a long time. I tried to capture the image of my children in their peaceful state. Their curled and sleeping bodies became blurry because of my tears.

"Goodbye for now, my beloved children," I said to them as they slept. "Your father is about to embark on a dangerous mission, and I hope that you will understand why I left you all, for the time being. I want to tell you that great achievement comes with an eminent sacrifice. I have such a substantial ambition. I desperately want for all of you to have a brighter future. I become valiant and confident to face the danger of what I am about to be involved in. I want to hold on to that bit of mysterious courage, which fortunately grew in me after the first treacherous escape attempt."

Despite the pouring rain, and with tiny luggage across my shoulder, I opened the door and left. I tried not to let anything hinder my decision. Why was it raining unusually heavily? I wondered if it was a sign—a warning from Heaven. With a few remaining ingot pieces sewn inside the inner linings of my coat, I walked fast in the heavy rain to the bus station. I began my journey to Cà Mau Peninsula at the most southern part of Vietnam.

Cà Mau Peninsula was known for its famous fishing and fish-sauce product. Many boats were built there every day. It was a land also famous for the big mosquitoes, which were known to carry and transmit dangerous diseases. I caught malaria the second day after I arrived in that infested land. Alone, sick, and surrounded by strangers, I left my fate in God's hand.

The first day I was in this infectious town, I ate at a street stall. I ordered a bowl of noodle soup. While quickly sipping noodles, I noticed an old man and a young boy. The old man only ordered one bowl of soup and watched the young boy eat. I offered to buy him a bowl. In the back of my mind, I guessed that he did not have enough money to buy himself one. I learned that his entire family had escaped. While running to the boat, he had gotten lost with his grandson. They had been left behind, and he had not heard from his family in about two months. He offered me a place to sleep at his house. The tiny house was built like a hut.

While I was sick, these strangers housed me, fed me, and nursed me back to my health. I managed to hide my gold, safe inside the lining of my coat. I got to know the old man. His name was Bảy Thọ, and he found out about my intentions. He recommended that I go to Thốt Nốt and meet his nephew, who would know a way to build a boat. He gave me the address and wrote a letter for me to give to his nephew. I found out that, in this land, it was not that difficult to obtain a permit to for a merchant boat. Going to Thốt Nốt and building a boat, I realized that I needed help from people I could trust.

I took the bus to Saigon, and from there I traveled home to my wife and my children. As the bus started to climb up the steep stretches of the road, my heart started to beat faster. I felt that my heart was trying to race across the hills and mountains. I was going home to my children with a secret and dangerous plan.

I had to keep my plan a top secret for the safety of the family. I felt the excitement mix with the happiness of seeing my family again, which created a mysterious thrill. The bus finally arrived at the station near the main supermarket in Đà Lạt. I walked home. It was pouring rain again. This time, I had no raincoat. I kept walking and felt nothing of this heavy rain. My heart was light and warm with the thought of seeing my precious children, and again hearing their laughter. I arrived at the door, and realized that I had no house key. I knocked so hard on the steel doors, yelling loudly to beat the sound of the rain so my children could hear me. Finally, water-soaked from a mixture of the rain and my tears, I ran to my children's embrace.

That evening, after the happiest and warmest meal, I sat with all my children, who surrounded me. We cuddled each other on my bed. I told them about my secret, which I had to disguise as a new business venture. I told them about the big mosquitoes, which had tried to suck out all my blood, and how I had conquered the creatures and come home healthy in one piece. I told my children that I wanted to build a merchant boat. This new business would provide for the family. My young children were innocently curious. They asked when they could ride on the boat. They thought that I could be a cool captain. For a brief moment, my heart sank. Ironically, I could not tell them about the dangerous journey awaiting them. I hugged each of them. I felt that my older children knew that I had lied.

After a few days visiting at home, I knew that I had to leave for Thốt Nốt. I held a meeting with all my children. I often held a family meeting to announce important events, or to give my children advice. Family meetings somehow distinguished themselves instantly from playful evening gatherings the moment they were held. I immediately felt intense sadness. My children understood that it was not the time for storytelling or playing games.

I gathered my strength and requested that my third son quit school to go to Thốt Nốt with me, and help carry out the plan for the new family business. I explained that I could not do it alone. I needed help, and the fact was that I could only place my full trust in an immediate family member. Among my children, my third son resembled me the most. From the time he was young, I already felt his strong reflection of my character. My third son was seventeen at the time. It was too much of me to ask him to quit school and place a burden on his young shoulders. I often told my children that education was the most important tool in building a successful life. Yet, I had to tell my son to sacrifice it—to quit school. My son immediately accepted my request. He knew about my secret plan. He'd experienced the past failed and treacherous escape attempt. He understood what I was doing.

The next early morning, we left Đà Lạt. It was a foggy morning. Father and son walked in the heavy fog to the bus station. We walked in silence, yet we heard loud voices from our racing minds. As a father, I was momentarily embarrassed to realize that my son, instead of taking the path to school, had to follow me on this perilous path.

We arrived at Thốt Nốt and met the family of Bảy Thọ's nephew. The nephew had received a special permit to build a merchant boat. I left my third son to stay with the family, to help them build the boat. I went to Saigon and bought an old boat engine. We rebuilt the engine to complete the boat. I wanted to teach my third son everything about the boat, and most important of all, the engine. From rebuilding it, he knew how to work it and fix it if there was a problem.

The boat was a twenty-five-foot merchant boat. I had a scheme. I had planned to hide my family's intention of escaping Vietnam in this merchant boat. My son and I would navigate this boat from Cà Mau to Vũng Tàu and along the Mekong River. The boat transported sand from Vũng Tàu to Cà Mau and watermelon from Cà Mau to Vũng Tàu. The boat also carried pots, fish sauces, and various produce to sell at many ports along the long stretch of this river. I wanted my son to know everything about life on the water and everything about this boat with its rebuilt engine.

The boat was equipped with a basic living cabin. In this boat and this small cabin, I carefully carried out my secret plan. I left my son to navigate the boat and dock it at Vũng Tàu, where I traveled to Saigon, Đà Lạt to carry out the scheme. I contacted my distant cousin, who used to be a captain of an American Navy ship. He had just gotten released from the communist political-reform prison. He also wanted to arrange for his family to escape Vietnam.

It took more than a year to carry out the plan. I needed this much time to prepare for the escape. I was able to gather some people who also wanted to escape. Those people agreed to share the cost of running this pretend business. The communist government set up many boat-inspection stations at every port along the Mekong River. Every time a boat passed through an inspection station, the boat owner had to pay a certain amount of money to continue the journey. It was called a "merchant boat fee." It was just another scheme to fill their greed. Boat merchants were never able to make any profit.

I taught my son to master the business. I trained him to

skillfully navigate the boat through rough water. He would be a second captain when this boat embarked on the perilous escape. We took a pretend fishing trip to test the boat in the ocean. We endured every fierce inspection from the communist officials. We had to bribe them and be constantly bullied by them. We survived each day. Together, as father and son, we did not let anger and anxiety dictate us. We buried our deep secret in our daily responsibilities. The goal was that, someday, we would be able to escape from it all. We held on to the hope that priceless freedom was awaiting us across the Pacific Ocean.

6

1983
THE SECOND ESCAPE
WAVING GOODBYE TO
MY SIX OLDER CHILDREN
FOR THE FINAL TIME

I FINALLY DECIDED ON THE ESCAPE DAY: MAY 19, 1983. May was the month in which the wind and Pacific Ocean would be considerately calm. My oldest daughter had recently married, and with a young family, had decided to stay behind and continue living in our home in Đà Lạt. I arranged for my wife and my eight other children to stay at a hotel in Saigon. My third son and my distance cousins stayed with the boat and waited for us. The boat was anchored where part of the Mekong River met the Pacific Ocean. It was near Vũng Tàu.

I had arranged to pay all the officials so they would stay away from the area. It was also arranged that the coastguards would be out of our sights. Again, escapees would be divided into small groups. Each small group had a leader who would direct them to either a canoe or taxi boat. Mekong River had many canals with shallow water. Canoe and small taxi boats were the convenient transportation method along the narrow and shallow waterways. I instructed my son to make sure all family members were on the boat before its anchor was raised. When everyone was on board, my son would strip the license plate off the boat, tie it to a rock, and throw it into the river to destroy the boat's identity.

After all the tough times preparing for this perilous journey, I came to make a fatal decision. Two years later, the consequences of this decision caught up with me.

It was previously planned that I would escape with my wife and nine of my children on the boat. Somehow, it turned out that only my six children would escape. My mind had been fooling me. Perhaps, with years of mental pressure, planning the escape in secret and in distress, and the high degree of responsibility got the best of me. Why did that decision creep into my mind at that time? The fatal decision was that only my six older children would escape. My wife and I and my three youngest children would stay behind.

I had seen many fellow boat owners who had the same goal as mine. Their families got thrown into prison due to their unsuccessful escapes. No one could bail them out. There was no one who remained outside of the prison to arrange to bribe the officials to bring them out of prison. All their assets were confiscated. When they came out of the prison, their houses and lands were already taken away. They became criminals and were thrown into the so-called economic-reformed land. There was a case when an entire family committed suicide. I became frightened of the thought of my entire family getting thrown into prison. This took over my thoughts.

My oldest daughter would not be capable of dealing with all the evils of the system. I would not want her to bear the immense responsibilities. Perhaps, I did not want her to bear the aftermath of a failed scheme. Its consequences would be too difficult to resolve.

It was finally decided, between my wife and me, that only my six older children would escape. My wife, my youngest three children, and I would stay behind. There were quite a few relatives who also wanted to escape. I entrusted my six older children to their care and decided to stay behind. Why did I do that? I can only give myself one answer: It was fate!

The morning of the escape, I rented a bicycle from the hotel and rode to the port where my third son stayed with the boat. I saw my obedient son from a distance. I left the bicycle and climbed up the steps to get to the boat. My legs wanted to stop, to hide my presence from my son. My heart sank, seeing his dark-tanned, skinny figure standing on the boat. I stopped and hid my presence from him, to wipe away the tears behind my dark sunglasses. I hesitated to tell him. However, I gathered my strength to reach the top of the boat, and I told him about the change of plan. My third son did not say much. Tears were flowing down his cheeks. From his eyes, I knew that he wanted to go against my decision. An invisible force made us stay silent in our thoughts.

Finally, I kissed him on his forehead and reminded him to remember all my instructions. I took the bicycle and left the boat. I rode the bicycle on the paved road, while my son drove the boat along the Mekong River. My son watched me; I watched him until both our sights faded and disappeared in the far distance. It was the last time that I saw my third son as a living father.

It was very humid that afternoon, in the heavily populated city of Saigon. I reached the hotel and instructed my older children, three brothers, and two sisters to leave and board the bus from Saigon to Vũng Tàu. I discreetly followed them with my bicycle. When they were all on the bus and ready to leave, I secretly and quickly waved goodbye to them. It was my last goodbye and the last time that I saw them. I drove the bicycle as far as I could behind the bus. I stopped and saw my children's images fade in the distance.

After they left, I waited for the news. That time, waiting to hear back from them, was such a torturous time of my life. I began to question myself as to why I had put my children in such peril. They could vanish in the ocean due to my decision. I could have sent my children to their deaths in the hope that they could find freedom across the Pacific Ocean. The realizations, the imaginations, crept up to me. Each day, each night ... became endless in the desperation of hearing back from them.

As a father, what had I done? I felt guilty!

As a father, how could I not be there to protect my children? I was disgusted with myself!

What happened if they were attacked by Thai pirates? They were murderous and extremely evil! I had, so many times, instructed my son to navigate the boat avoiding the ocean near Thai Lan Bay. Did they take that path? I hoped they did not!

What if the engine stopped, and my son could not fix it?

I had equipped the boat with a spare engine!

What if the food ran out? I had packed the boat with rice, dried squid, dried fish ... more than a month's supply of food!

What if the water ran out? I had even packed lemon juice, with a huge tank of fresh water!

What if they got lost and ran out of fuel? I had equipped the boat with the navy compass and enough fuel to reach Singapore!

What if the storm sank the boat? I had checked the calm weather of May numerous times!

My head echoed with what if ... and what if ...

As a father, what had I done?

My mind became darkened with numerous negative and weary thoughts.

I was devastated. Burned out.

Then luckily, and finally, I learned that their escape was a success! Roughly a month after they escaped, I got the news that they had arrived safely at a refugee camp, located on a small island of Indonesia. My heart was about to be burst with relief. I was still a father, and I became alive again.

7

1985
THE THIRD ESCAPE
I BEGIN MY LIFE AS A GHOST

HOW CAN I BEGIN? IT IS HARD TO write down what really happened. The decision of not escaping as a whole family back in 1983 became a fatal one two years later. It was the main reason that I was stuck here in Vietnam for two more years. There is no answer as to why I decided to try another escape. I could have waited a few more years to leave Vietnam legally. Looking back, as a ghost, I had to say that it was fate. My time was up in the book of Heaven. Along with my nine-year-old, youngest daughter, circumstances happened that led to my last day as a human being on this earth.

Ironically, I held the sponsorship papers that had been sent to me from my children, who had already settled in Canada, at the time of this fatal escape. After staying more than a year in the Indonesian refugee camp, they'd left for Canada. They were sponsored by the Mountain Fund to Help the Boat People Group, located in Hamilton, Ontario.

They became immigrants awaiting to become Canadian citizens. They got jobs to support themselves, and the younger ones were in high school. They'd worked hard to get the sponsorship papers for their father, their mother, and their three youngest brothers and sister as soon as they could.

Back in Vietnam, the communist government gave me an even harder time. I could not stay in Đà Lạt, since they threatened that they would put me in prison. Technically, I became a criminal and was being investigated for having six children in Canada. My two youngest sons and my youngest daughter could not attend school. My remaining small family had to move numerous times, from place to place, to avoid getting caught by the communist government. They had exhausted my resources waiting it out. I could not even submit the sponsorship papers to migrate to Canada. I was turning sixty, and I became anxious with impatience.

I secretly came back to Đà Lạt by myself to pay the last visit to my oldest daughter, whose family still lived in our home. It was also raining very hard on that day. I waited for the rain to stop and took refuge at a Buddhist temple near my house. A few years back, I would have walked in this pouring rain. This time, I did not want to at all, even though it was only a short distance from the temple to my home. The head monk from the temple offered me some tea, and strangely, he also offered me some prayers. I left the temple when the heavy rain stopped. I took it as a hint that my time on earth was near its end. Somehow, I still wanted to proceed with my risky decision. That evening, I cuddled my three grandchildren for the last time.

A day before that fatal day, or a day before I died, my wife and I and my three young children left Saigon for Bà Rịa, Vũng Tàu. We were directed to hide in a chicken farmhouse and wait until it was dark. Then night came, and the owner of the house told us it was time to leave. A man came and guided us to follow him through bushes and small farmhouses. The dogs barked constantly and echoed through the fields. Along the way in the dark of the night, many other groups of escapees gathered to walk the same path. Suddenly, we heard a scream and people started running. I stopped running and led my family to hide under a big willow tree with a few other escapees. We heard some gunshots in the distance. Under the willow tree, we stayed silently in fear of being caught. My youngest daughter cried silently when fire ants bit her. I felt a strange fear in me.

The paternal instinct in me foreshadowed that something was wrong. I could just take my wife and my children back to Saigon. However, I could not prevent what was coming next. I felt vulnerable and confused. I could not control my thoughts to act on my instinct. My family and I kept following the other escapees, continuing to run after the leader of the groups told us it was safe to continue the walk.

We were then instructed to run through vast fields of mud to get to the small riverboat, which would take us to a bigger boat near the ocean. I started to realize what my six older children had been through two years before. They had probably hidden in the chicken farmhouse and run through these muddy fields. While running, my youngest son got his feet stuck in the mud. It turned out that he had tied his shoes too tight, and his feet were filled with heavy mud, and they were trapped. I used both my lighter and the cigarettes to burn the shoestrings to free his feet.

We finally arrived at the river bank and walked through shallow water to get to the awaiting canoes and taxi boats. They transported us to a bigger boat near the ocean, with more than two hundred other escapees. The boat was over-crowded. Escapees were fighting for space on the boat. It was too late for me to take my family back to land. No one was allowed to leave the big boat. People were suspicious that those who left would then notify the policemen to arrest the other escapees.

The boat departed at dawn. The engine started, and the boat was moving slowly. Something held the boat from moving faster. It moved very slow, fighting a force that kept pulling it back. It turned out that, in chaos and fear, no one had raised the anchor and let it drag while the boat was departing. The boat dragged the anchor a short distance, until the rope that was tied to it came loose. The anchor stayed behind, under the river near the ocean. The overcrowded and anchorless boat drove for a few hours and reached the sea territory of Côn Sơn Island.

It was a belief that the anchor needed to stay with the boat. A boat without its anchor would not be able to complete its journey. Therefore, many peoples on the boat were very upset, learning that the anchor was left behind. It was already an unlucky sign.

It was near the evening, but the anchorless boat had still not reached the international sea waters to feel safe. The sky slowly became dark. As the boat was moving, many dolphins suddenly appeared and swam along the sides of the boat. This was known to be a bad omen, another unlucky sign!

Many people on the boat started to chant their prayers, and said that the dolphins were driven by dead spirits, which followed the boat—the spirits of other escapees who'd drowned while fleeing Vietnam like us. These miserable spirits would pull the boat down into the ocean to join them. My wife lit incense and prayed with my children. The dolphins suddenly dove under, and the fearful sight of them was gone. We thought that the bad omen had left ... that the wretched spirits had probably gone away.

The sky became black and covered with a thick dark cloud. The boat suddenly stalled! Its propeller was caught in a big fishing net. The captain of the boat tried to maneuver it out; however, the boat kept moving in a circle. As it moved strangely in this way, more of the fishing net became stuck around the boat. Bloody seawater started to creep up, surrounding the boat. People started to scream. The fish died in the net, and their bloody bodies started to circle along with the boat. The atmosphere became eerie. The dolphins appeared again to feast on the dead fish. People cried and screamed louder for the boat to stop circling.

The fishermen's boat appeared from a distance and quickly caught up with us. They were friendly at first but got very angry seeing that their net and their catch of the day had been destroyed. They intended to rescue their net from being further sabotaged by the overly crowded boat. They threw ropes, tied our boat to theirs, and pulled. People on the boat started to get agitated. Some screamed out loud to increase the chaos level. The fishermen got very angry and used the radio to signal the police boat to come.

The police boat appeared from afar. It did not take long

for us to see it. The fishermen started to argue amongst one another. They decided to cut the ropes and drive away. The moment they cut the rope, the escape boat became unbalanced and tilted to the side. I looked into the cabin, and it was empty. There was no one to control the boat from the wheel. The captain had already jumped into the ocean to avoid being caught by the policemen. A few shots were fired from the police boat.

People frantically fought among themselves for life jackets, cursed, and jumped into the ocean. The boat tilted more and more to the side. Women, men, and children screamed. The screaming and the crying mixed together with the high-pitch, harsh-edged, squeaky sound of the dolphins and sucked the fear out of every human. The dreadful atmosphere announced that death had finally arrived.

I huddled my crying wife and my children to me. My chest started to hurt. My one and only working eye started to see double vision. I tried to remain calm and quickly got a hold of a life jacket. Sadly, it was the only one for four people. The fishing boat turned back to the rescue, since they saw the escaping boat slowly sinking, and that people were dying. I quickly tied the life jacket to my two sons and told them to jump. They were so scared. They trembled, and their tiny bodies were shaking in distress. They hesitated and kept on crying and calling out for me. I had no other choice.

I told them my last words: "I am very sorry. Stop crying and save yourselves. Remember to stick together! Close your eyes and quickly jump. Please, sons, listen to me. Jump and keep on swimming to that fishing boat."

The two brothers did not even move an inch. They cried

louder and remained in dismay. I finally picked both of them up and threw them into the ocean with the last life jacket. My youngest daughter and my wife were clinging on to me, again crying out loud. The boat tilted even more. Seawater started to fill the boat. The boat sunk faster. People screamed and helplessly wailed. I panicked even more, but caught a glimpse of my two young sons moving in the seawater.

The boat started to make a cracking sound, continuously tilting. In a desperate moment, I held both my daughter and my wife tightly and did not know what to do next. The boat now flipped quickly, and we all fell into the water. I lost control of my arms and felt that my daughter had slipped away from me, but somehow, she was able to cling onto the boat. In the chaos, I grabbed on to a broken wooden board to stay afloat, and managed to hold on to my wife. My wife did not know how to swim. I tried to kick my legs and kept her head above the seawater. I also looked and called out for my daughter. I swallowed seawater while I was screaming her name. My chest hurt. Then I felt my last energy. I vaguely heard my youngest daughter calling and crying out for me, her father! I saw the blurry image of her small hands trying to reach me and then disappearing under the sea water. I did not see or hear from my youngest daughter again!

Oh God, what had I done? My chest hurt again. I felt a sharp pain in my heart. I gathered all my strength and pushed my wife a short distance along the waves towards the fishing boat. My whole body became stiff. I could not swim or move anymore. My mouth filled with salty and bloody water. Everything started to turn black. I could feel that the oxygen was refusing to enter my lungs. I tried, but I could not breathe. I felt so light. I lost my vision in my one and only functional eye. Everything went completely black. Then, suddenly, I felt that I could fly. I could see again. I saw the light, and I saw God at the door of Heaven...

8

FAREWELL
MY BELOVED DAUGHTER

I WAS DEAD! I WAS SIXTY YEARS OLD. The fishermen's boat threw out the rest of their fishing nets to rescue my two sons, my wife, and other escapees. My lifeless body and other dead people were also recovered and placed on either the fishermen's boat or the police boat. They transported both the dead and living people to Côn Sơn Island. My youngest daughter was trapped and drowned with the sinking boat. She was only nine years old.

A short moment before, we had been crying with each other. Now, we comforted each other as ghosts floating above the waves that submerged the sunken boat.

I whispered to her,

"My dearest daughter, I am very sorry; I could not save you."

She turned and gave me a gentle smile,

"But we are still together, Dad!"

I explained to her, "We are together in death."

Suddenly, I started to realize that I could not see my daughter clearly.

Her voice faded. I could not hear what she was trying to say. She let go of my hand and started to disappear slowly.

Selfishly, I said to her, "Dearest daughter, do not leave me alone! Please stay with me!"

I could not grasp onto her. She could not call me anymore. It was her time to completely depart from this earth.

God had taken her innocent soul to Heaven!

9

CÔN SƠN ISLAND
A LONELY SOUL

MY WIFE AND MY SONS WERE RELEASED AFTER three months in the Côn Sơn Prison. Along with others, they were transported back to the mainland. During the time that my wife and my sons were held in prison, I was with them. I followed them every step they took. I wrapped around them every night as they slept. I tried to comfort them every time they cried. They mentally suffered beyond what I could describe. Despite what I tried, I was only a ghost and invisible to them. They felt nothing of my existence. Their every day was a struggle to stay alive in a dirty, crowded prison. Prisoners cursed each other, fought over sleeping places, water, and food. My wife became very ill, and they were released early due to her health issue.

I could not follow my wife and my sons to the mainland. A mysterious force had exerted on me to prevent me from freely moving off of this island. While living, during the ancestral memorial, I'd heard that the soul had to stay with the dead body for a certain period of time. As a ghost, my soul kept lingering near my dead body, which decomposed quickly beneath the ground. My wife was smart to bury me without the plastic bag. I wandered aimlessly on the island, unable to be free of the burial site.

Côn Sơn Island had many prisons built with torturing quarters. Before 1975, it had been used to house notorious criminals. It was also used for torturing and killing many communist prisoners. It was now deserted and occasionally held escaping boat people who were captured in the sea near the island. There were many abandoned prisons. Many nameless tombstones were scattered all over the island. Many hidden mass graves waited to be discovered.

Not being able to free my soul from this island, I came to absorb that it was the most regretful and sorrowful time of my life as a ghost.

I wandered the stretches of the isolated beaches of this island, listening to the sound of the roaring waves from dusk to dawn. I felt the loneliness of the sound. It also expressed the sadness of its surroundings. Elsewhere on the earth, the beach could have human footprints. Seagulls flew above the waves to search for food. The oceans and their beaches had their life. The sound of the ocean could soothe a human mind. Here, on this island, there were isolated and nameless tombstones ... fruitless and broken palm trees.

The sound of the waves meeting the sand on this island expressed the regret of mistakes that could not be undone. The sound of the waves exposed sorrow that could never be cured. I named this island the regretful lands, with never-ending unhappiness.

I heard the weary cries of many dead people who had died unjust deaths. Their souls longed for the living to come to this island, to discover and collect their corpses. They dreamt of proper burial ceremonies, close to their living families.

My flesh quickly decomposed into the best compost to feed the land. Grass started to grow on top of my grave and quickly spread to become a vast and tall grass field. The grass grew so tall that no one, from a distance, could imagine or even recognize that it had once been the burial site of my lonely soul.

10

1986
LEAVING CÔN SƠN ISLAND

MY BODY STAYED IN THE GROUND BELOW THOSE tall grasses for more than one year. My soul slowly became weary. I longed for the time that I could be with my family, who had settled on two continents. I wanted to protect my children even in my death. During the loneliest time, I reminded myself that forever departing from this world would have to wait.

My wife finally came back to the island with my nephew-in-law. I learned that my wife had recovered from major surgery to regain her health. With a connection from her younger brother, who knew some top communist officials, she was able to make the trip to the island by the helicopter. When they first arrived, all they saw was the vast field of tall grasses. My wife was really worried and disappointed. They had a hard time finding my grave in the short allotted time. They had to go back to the mainland due to the tight schedule of the helicopter.

My wife and my nephew-in-law stayed with my distance cousin's wife in Saigon to wait for the second trip. From there, they were transported to Côn Sơn Island again by helicopter. They were finally able to have a full-day trip. I knew that my wife would have to pay for all the cost. There were no hidden gold ingots left. Money had been sent from my children who lived in Canada.

The helicopter dropped them off on the island on an early morning. The sky was clear, and the sun came and brought bright sunshine to the island. They searched in the roots of the grass to find a circle of stones. They were the marks my wife had set more than a year earlier, to find my grave. No human was messing with the land; only nature would change it. After hours of examining numerous areas of this vast grassy field, they still could not locate my burial site.

Around noon, in frustration, my nephew-in-law lit incense and called out loud for me. His voice was fiercely echoed by the mountains of the deserted island. Only the two of them were in this part of the vast land. Both were desperate to find my grave.

My soul was around them, seeing their every move. Yet, I could not speak. I could not express how happy I was to see their presence. I could not yell out loud where my grave was located. I could not hug my wife. I was helplessly invisible to them.

My nephew-in-law later told his family that he felt my presence as a ghost, and that it was my spirit that had led him to the exact location of my burial site. He traced the pattern of the setting stones. He knew it, and he started to work. He cut the tall grass to further investigate the stone pattern. He then anxiously and quickly dug. While digging, he said his heart raced with the speed of his hand. His sweat combined with his tears when he finally reached my bones. My wife asked him to check under my feet. They found the black plastic bag. My wife then knew for sure that it was the exact grave, since she had rolled my body bag and placed it under my feet to purposely mark the body. She wept while recognizing the clothes that I had worn when she buried me. What remained of the light blue shirt and the black pair of pants were now loosely mixed with dirt, sand, and my bones.

My nephew-in-law carefully picked up every single piece of my bones and placed them in a small wooden coffin. He started with my skull and moved to my feet. That way he would be sure not to miss any. My wife was a nurse. She knew the order of the bones, and what bones would stay intact, to count them correctly. My nephew-in-law worked non-stop. He hurried and wanted to finish the task so badly. The pilot and the helicopter could only wait for them for so long.

When most of my bones were collected, the heavy rain suddenly came. The rain was pouring faster and harder. My wife and my nephew-in-law had to stop, and hurried back to the spot where the helicopter was waiting for them. My nephew-in-law could not collect my toe bones. He did not have enough time. The rain came faster than he could imagine. The toe bones were too small and had been quickly buried in the pool of muddy water. Water and dirt mixed instantly and hid the presence of the tiny bones.

I did not mind not having my toe bones in my coffin. I was grateful knowing that my wife had found my body and arranged to bring my remains to Đà Lạt. While living, I considered myself as an adventurous man. I concluded that my toe bones had stayed in this land as a testament to my significant time spent on this island.

My nephew-in-law later recalled the event, and said that he was very scared while digging and collecting my remains. He felt a chill running down his spine the whole time, despite the fact that it was a very hot day and he was under the direct sun. He recalled how I had helped and cared for his family in a hard time. After 1975, he had been imprisoned due to the political reform. He wanted to repay my kindness. He felt awful for not being able to collect my toe bones. He said that he dug his hand under the pool of water and dirt, but strangely, could not feel any hard objects. It felt like the bones were hiding away from him.

My coffin was transported to the mainland by the helicopter. My wife and my nephew-in-law brought my coffin to a cremation centre. My wife did not want to cremate me. She arranged to completely dry my bones to disinfect them. She then placed all the pieces of my bones into a small travel bag. From Saigon, she and my nephew-in-law would travel to Đà Lạt by bus. She had to hide my bones in this travel bag without anyone knowing. People were very superstitious. They would not want any dead people travelling with them on the bus. It would bring bad luck or even death to the passengers on the bus. Hiding the fact that dead bones were in the travel bag was the only way she would be able to board the bus to Đà Lạt.

11

DU SINH CEMETERY
MY SECOND FUNERAL

MY WIFE LEFT MY NEPHEW-IN-LAW AT THE BUS station when they arrived at Đà Lạt. She went straight to the Linh Sơn Buddhist temple, located a very short distance from my home. Most Buddhist temples in Vietnam had a separate building, which acted as a morgue to contain dead bodies before the funeral. She had arranged with the head monk to place my bones in the temple morgue. It was also a superstition that a dead body could not be placed in the home. It would bring bad omens or bad luck to the family. It was also suspected that the dead would attract the living and eventually take his or her life.

My bones were once again being exposed to the air. The head monk consciously took my bones out of the travel bag and wrapped them in red cloth. He placed a white band around the forehead of my skull. My mother was still alive at that time of my death, and it was a tradition that, even in death, I would still have to mourn her death when her time came. He lit incense and chanted the Buddhist scriptures for three days. He was praying for my soul to be free from this earth.

He did not know that I had defied the process. I had left so much undone. My responsibilities, as a father to my nine surviving children, were unfinished. I wanted to be a filial son to my mother. Yet, I had died before her. My living youngest son was only thirteen years old. I wanted to reunite the family. I wanted to see Canada and America. I wanted to exercise my business ambition in the lands of opportunities. I could not depart from the living world. Yet, I'd had to die in desperation to save my wife and my youngest daughter. How could I leave this world? I desperately wanted to live, but I could only remain between life and death.

Du Sinh cemetery was new. The communist government had recently assigned the land as the new burial sites. It consisted of stretches of steep hills. My wife came to see a monk who was a master in reading people's past lives. She hoped that the monk could communicate with me to choose my best burial spot on this hill. Many people said that the monk had the gift of being able to communicate with the dead. He lived alone near the hills and rarely interacted with anyone. The head monk of Linh Sơn Buddhist temple told him to meet with my wife. The head monk of Linh Sơn temple remembered me. We had shared a cup of tea and prayer the last time I had visited my oldest daughter's family. I'd guessed at that time that he had seen into my future and knew that my death was awaiting me.

My spirit was following my wife the entire time I was back in Đà Lạt. When she met with the monk who could communicate with the dead, he told her that I was sitting right beside her. My wife trembled with fear. Adding to her dismay, he told her that I was very pleased that my bones had been brought back to this land. My toe bones were still at the Côn Sơn Island, and it was meant to be so. The monk then went to Du Sinh cemetery. He lit a few incenses and placed them on the spot near the top the hill.

The day of my second funeral arrived. Again, this time, I was buried without any of my children. Only my wife and the cemetery workers were present. My wife strongly believed in the theory that the dead would pull the living into their deadly world. The head monk of Linh Sơn Buddhist temple came to my home and chanted Buddhist scriptures. While my sons and my oldest daughter remained at home, my tiny coffin was lowered into the ground of the hill. My younger sons then rode their bicycles to visit the burial site, after all the dirt had covered my grave. Standing beside my new grave, they wept more, and my wife wept less.

I wanted to compare my wife to a cactus. The cactus did not have leaves. Its leaves had evolved to spines to adapt to its environment. The spines of the cactus were evolved from leaves to prevent water from evaporating in the hot weather of the desert. My wife had been through so much suffering, both mentally and physically. She had to adapt to live on. She appeared cold from the outside, but inside, she was full of the tears she had been holding in.

My body stayed in Du Sinh cemetery for twenty-nine years. My tombstone was beautifully designed and situated near the top of the hill. Underneath the hill, more streets were constructed, more houses were built, and more farms were cultivated. The living continued and so did the dead. More tombstones were placed in the cemetery. I had two children who passed away when they were young. Their remains were also moved from the Old Mã Thánh cemetery to Du Sinh cemetery to be reburied near mine. Only my youngest daughter did not have a grave.

Underneath that ground, my dead bones stayed silent, but my soul was disturbed. I learned that my family again faced a dreadful time by the communist government. Once in a while, an official or a policeman suddenly paid a visit to the house to criticize and condemn my family's sins—the sin of escaping the country—and how I had deserved to die. When I died, my body was pulled out of the water and transported to Côn Sơn Island by the police boat. On this boat, they took some photos of my dead body as the record. The photos were brought to Đà Lạt and then posted at the central police station. It was posted there to give a warning to the citizens of the tragic result of trying to escape the communist homeland. Each time they came to the house, my wife or my daughter had to bribe them. My death was exposed and also extorted.

WAR

CHIẾN TRANH

12

QUẢNG ĐỨC WAS A MOUNTAIN TOWN THAT BELONGED to Buôn Mê Thuột province. After 1975, its name was changed to Đắc Lák. The land bent westward towards Lao. It consisted of thick, untouched mountains populated by many wild animals. Yellow and white tigers ruled their forest with many monkeys. North Vietnamese soldiers, also known as Viet Cong, had many bases there. They built huts and caves along the edge of Buôn Ới River.

In 1961, I decided to bring my young family to this mountain. I left my hometown of Huế with my wife, our three oldest children, and my older brother's family. We heard that it was a land of new development, with opportunities for the construction business. My wealth was accumulated from this land. The westward stretch of mountains was the only land accessible to the south. The South Vietnamese soldiers needed this land for transportation. I entered a business venture with my older brother. We got a contract from the Americans to build roads, schools, a hospital, houses, and military barracks.

On this mountain, my young family was expanded with five more children, but I lost a son who was born in 1963 and a daughter who was born in 1967, due to the lack of a modern hospital and medicines. Our first home was burnt and destroyed due to American aircraft bombarding the Viet Cong huts north of Buôn Ối River. I was away on a business trip to Saigon and came home to a pile of ashes.

No words could describe how horrified I felt at that exact moment, seeing the devastating site. I found out that my wife and my children were staying with my older brother's family. My family was safe, due to the quick thinking of my wife. She had poured water on the mattress and put the children on it. She also covered them with wet blankets and pulled them out of the burning house. My wife told me that she had not liked the house anyway, which had become a central spot for the owls. They somehow liked our house and gathered on the roof at night. I did not mind, and the location of the house was by the river, where I took my oldest son fishing on less busy days. My wife said that omens came with the sound of the owls every night. Therefore, she had always been prepared for the worst situation.

I built another house next to my brother's family and moved my family there. The two houses were connected by an underground cave. The cave was an important component on the blueprint. The bombing from US aircraft was constant along the river. We often heard gunfights between the South Vietnamese soldiers and the Viet Cong. My children experienced the direct effect of war. Their sleep was constantly disturbed. They were often awakened in the middle of the night and slept in the underground cave. My third daughter hated the dark and cried every time. My wife sang for her to go to sleep. My older brother scolded his children to behave and to stay quiet.

I guarded the door and put on a courageous attitude every time. During those stressful nights, I always questioned if all the money was worth risking human lives. I reminded myself that living on this mountain was only temporary. Once I had enough money, I would take my family and leave this war-torn land.

The Americans paid me cash. After each deal was signed, I came home with a briefcase full of money. My third son ran out to happily greet me and carry the briefcase inside. Sometimes, the briefcase was heavier than his weight. He had to drag it along the floor. My wife sewed long, thin fabric tubes to store the money. We hid them within the wall. There was no bank to make deposits. On my business trips to Saigon, my wife would tie the tubes of money around my body, hidden under my thick clothes. I used the money to buy gold and brought it home. Again, my wife hid the gold within various walls of the house. Among my collection of cars, there was a Rolls Royce, several Dodge pickup trucks, a Jeep Cherokee, and a Chevrolet van. I often drove my young children to visit the construction sites in my favourite French-made automobile: a black Citroen Traction Avant.

The Quảng Đức town was developed and built with more houses, schools, a hospital, a town hall, and military bases. I built and opened a pharmacy for my wife to operate and to practice, since she was a nurse. I taught my children to cultivate lands and planted fruit and vegetables in the gardens surrounding the house. I brought seeds back from many of my business trips and guided my children to grow them. We also raised pigs for meat. During the intense bombing time, the American soldiers closed roads, schools, and supermarkets. The whole town was under curfew. During those hard times, my family harvested the fruits and lived off the vegetable garden.

One day, home again from a long business trip, I arrived home and found my children so sad and crying out to me. The whole garden was horribly destroyed. My wife was angry. My oldest son then told me the strangest story. The garden had been sabotaged by a school of monkeys, not by the war. There were banana trees in the garden. My children never had a chance to taste the first ripe banana. They had all been eaten by the monkeys. My oldest son came up with the idea of teaching them a lesson. He thought he could put red chili powder in the bananas to change their taste and scare the monkeys away. However, it turned out to be a disaster.

I pictured my children closing the doors and hiding inside the house, awaiting the monkeys' arrival, entering the trap. Brothers and sisters giggled and laughed with excitement. The monkeys feasted themselves on the bananas mixed with hot chili. Then they screamed, since their tongues were severely burned. They did not know to drink the water to clear the hot taste of the chili. They did not know what was going on. They shrieked and madly jumped up and down, running and wrecking everything around them. Some were lying down, holding their mouths and tummies and crying at the same time. Some monkey desperately licked the dirt on the ground to ease the pain on their tongues. The lesson to teach the monkey not to steal the bananas became a disaster. The excitement turned into a scary feeling. The monkeys then left the garden. However, shortly after, they came back to the garden with the entire school of angry monkeys. They wrecked the whole garden as an act of revenge.

I explained to my children that monkeys used to own these stretches of the westward land of Vietnam. Their habitat had been invaded by humans. In this war-infested land, it was not just human lives that were wasted or in misery, nature and animals also suffered.

I came to realize that, besides trying to build roads, houses, and developed villages on this land, the Americans could destroy them at any time. The bombings to sabotage the hidden caves of communist soldiers and Viet Cong took priority over the development of the land. I often had conflicted feelings as to what I was trying to achieve. In the end, it was all about survival and making lives better, in either the best or worst circumstances.

I employed many villagers, and many of them were also my wife's patients. They often paid her with eggs, chickens, and rice. One time, she was paid with a pet monkey. The monkey was trained to do light house chores. Due to the bad experience with the monkeys, my wife was prepared to give away this pet monkey at any time. My children were also not fond of the pet monkey. At one time, the monkey imitated my wife and chopped vegetables using the kitchen knife. My wife was horrified and told me to quickly bring the monkey to the deep forest. She was also fearful that the group of monkeys would come back to destroy the family garden again. I put the pet monkey onto my truck and drove to the edge of the forest. I let it go, but it found its way back to the house the same day.

The second time, I covered its eyes and drove a bit deeper into the forest. This time, it seemed to understand that it was not welcome in our home. Its wild instinct gave the animal a sense of the freedom awaiting it ahead. It jumped off my truck, yelled out a strange sound, and disappeared into the forest. I stood beside the truck and lit a cigarette. I breathed in the nicotine and breathed out its smoke. My thoughts flowed with the smoke, which traveled with the wind into the deep mountains. In this rare moment of solitude, I recalled that my mother had once told me that I bore the spirit of the tiger. I was born in the year of the tiger. She believed that I was compatible with the mountain. My business ambition was successful in this land. I was turning forty, and I was a millionaire.

ANCHORLESS

13

THE MOUNTAIN AND ITS TIGER

TIGERS RULE THE MOUNTAIN AND IS CONSIDERED THE king of the forest in Vietnamese culture. Vietnam had a large population of yellow tigers. White tigers were rare, but once in a while, they were spotted by the helicopters. Land mines and chemical bombs destroyed the richness of the mountain, and many villagers were killed by the tigers coming out from the deep woods. Dirt roads were built across the forest near the river for transportation. Tiger traps were set along the river. Bridges were also quickly built to cross large creeks. The creeks were the central gathering spots for many tigers to drink the water. The fierce animal could hide at the edge of the forest and suddenly appear to hunt its prey.

I remembered that full-moon evening. I was driving home from inspecting a construction site. The schedule was delayed, and I could not finish until late in the evening. The main roads were again closed due to the spotting of a Viet Cong during the day. The militaries and law-enforcement officers were dispatched to pursue the Viet Cong. I decided to take the dirt roads along the edge of the forest, near the river.

This road led through a shallow creek. My jeep suddenly stalled on the bridge, with steam escaping through the engine cover. I stepped out of the vehicle and opened the hood to let out the steam. I took buckets and went down to the creek to get some water to cool down the engine. In a hurry to get home, I did not think twice of stepping down the steep dirt road to the shallow creek. The full moon was bright to guide my path. I got the water and carried it to my jeep. When I was near the jeep, I saw a huge tiger move slowly and hop into the top of the vehicle. My eyes met the wild eyes of the king of the forest. It was a miracle that the animal just sat still and looked straight at me.

My instinct told me to hit the animal with the water buckets. The water splashed on both the animal and onto the hot engine. The clanking sounds of the falling metal buckets against the vehicle echoed to break the eerie silence of the mountain. The wild animal jumped off and hit the engine cover to make it suddenly drop closed.

I quickly jumped into my jeep, shut the door, and started the engine. I applied full pressure to the gas pedal and swirled the steering wheel vigorously out of sight of the angry animal. I closed my eyes for a moment and kept driving straight. I heard its roar and felt a chill running down my spine. Through the mirrors, I saw the huge animal run after its prey. I prayed to Amithaba Buddha for her mercy to bring me home safe to my children. I drove as if I could win a gold medal for auto racing. Finally, the fearful sight of the tiger was far in the distance. It decided to stop pursuing its prey.

That evening, I was shaken. I told my family about the close encounter with the king of the mountain. My wife was horrified, and my children screamed in hearing the experience. With time, however, it became a story often told at bedtime. My third daughter kept asking me to retell the story many times. She was fascinated by hearing how my eyes and the tiger's had met each other. Yet, in that brief moment, nothing had happened. I was born in the year of the tiger. Perhaps, it was true that I held the spirit of a tiger. I told my daughter that the tiger recognized me as one of its kind. It did not attack me right away. In that rare and lucky moment, I could quickly react and escape such danger.

The experience shaped my thoughts regarding my fate. In encountering the tiger, I did not die, yet I died in the ocean. At that time, death had not yet been sent to meet me. My time in the book of Heaven had not yet arrived. It was written that I had to die in the peaceful Pacific Ocean, not in the chaos of war and not in the forest filled with fierce animals.

14

1971
LEAVING QUẢNG ĐỨC

THE NIGHT I ENCOUNTERED THE TIGER, MY WIFE also faced a dangerous situation. She was inside the kitchen, and the back door was open. She was making dinner and cooking food for the pigs at the same time. We never wasted any food. Any unused food, we boiled on a stone stove outside the house and fed to the pigs.

A stranger who wore dirty black shirt and pants suddenly appeared and asked for some foods. He had his face hidden under a straw hat and a black scarf. My wife ran out of the kitchen into the living room to check on my children, screaming for them to hide from this fearful sight. The man quickly turned to the pot for the food belonging to the pigs. He immediately sat down and ate right from the pot, and then left. It turned out that he was the Viet Cong who had been spotted and was being hunted by the South Vietnamese soldiers that evening. My wife never revealed his appearance to the policemen. She told the children to stay quiet about the event.

Sadly, he was caught and shot dead. His shallow grave was dug up, and his body was eaten by wild animals. He had only come to my house to ask for food. He was probably very hungry to risk his life coming out of his hiding cave. Tragically, his last meal was probably pig food. Even though he was a Viet Cong, he was my fellow countryman, a Vietnamese! The war revealed its ugliest sights and in various ironic forms.

Money was made and could soon be gone. I suffered a huge loss to my business. We needed cement and bricks to build, and often acquired them from Saigon. The building materials were transported to Quảng Đức by mid-size trucks. Land mines were exploded and destroyed the main routes to the town. The paths were closed and needed to be prepared. I hired military planes to transport the trucks full of the materials to meet the building deadline. While the plane was flying in the air, the signal for the engine in one of the wings indicated malfunction. The weight was too much to land safely. To save human lives, the pilot opened the back of the plane and dumped all the trucks into the ocean. I lost all the materials and one of the most profitable contracts.

In this war-infested land, I accumulated my gold. My young family grew. However, all came with a price. I caught eye disease, and lacking modern healthcare, I lost the vision in my right eye. I also lost one son and one daughter to illness. Again, I blamed the lack of advanced medicines. I often wondered, had lived in a bigger city such as Saigon, if my eye would have been cured. Would my son and my daughter have survived their illnesses?

Hiding in the underground family cave was constant,

and hearing about the lives which were lost almost every day. Thinking about losing our homes from bombings made daily survival more mentally difficult. One could easily lose his or her mind. It happened to my older brother. He was always fearful. Adding to his stress, he lost his oldest son in a motorcycle accident. He was devastated from the loss. His mind was gone. He had no energy left to continue operating the business with me. We both knew that we needed to leave this land. My older brother abandoned the business and his family house and left for Đà Lạt.

My decision to leave this land was finalized in 1971. I sent my three older children to live with my wife's younger brother in Đà Lạt first. Everything was cheaply sold or given away.

My wife pretended to be pregnant to have enough room to hide all the gold around her fake-pregnant tummy. Gold ingots were also sewed inside the lining of our coats. I hired a military plane to leave Quảng Đức with my wife, my four younger children, and my green jeep.

15

1975
TURBULENT TIMES

WAR FINALLY ARRIVED AT ĐÀ LẠT ON AN unusually hot day at the beginning of April 1975. The communist soldiers had captured most of the cities and towns near Đà Lạt. Many people had left their homes and moved to Saigon, which was still controlled by the South Vietnamese government. The sky was very clear, and many helicopters hovered over the soccer field near Xuân Hương Lake. South Vietnamese soldiers were deployed into Đà Lạt to protect the city. That day, all schools had closed early, and my third son and third daughter, who attended the same school, did not come home at their usual time.

My third son and third daughter attended a French public school, which was about a half-an-hour drive from our home. A man who lived in the neighborhood had a van and started the business of picking up children before school and dropping them off after school. My children were among other children in the neighborhood to use his service. That day, I was waiting anxiously for them, but they did not come home. I decided to walk to the driver's house to find out what happened. He told me that he had driven to the school but could not wait for my children and had left, because the South Vietnamese soldiers had put up the sign to close off some streets near the school. He'd had to leave before he was trapped with other children. I was so angry, and I could not control my temper. Before I could pour my anger onto him, he ran off through the back door of his house. I tried to be calm myself, to figure out a way to find my children.

My wife and all my children were home except for the brother and sister. I hoped that they would hide somewhere in the school and wait for me. I drove my jeep to school. The streets to the school were, in fact, closed by the military. I could not pass them to find my children. I was ordered by soldiers who carried guns to go home, and they warned me not to drive my jeep around the city. I drove back home and got onto my bicycle. I asked my first son to go look for them using a bicycle as well. We circled the opened streets, among other people who also frantically rushed home or looked for their children from other schools.

After a long and peaceful time, this small city on top of a plateau was facing the reality of war. The people had not prepared for it. Many peoples who lived in the centre of the city closed their businesses and left for Saigon. That day, the people from the opened supermarket had to close up everything and were forced to leave. People who lived far from the centre of the cities waited it out in their own homes. South Vietnamese soldiers guarded the streets to prevent looting and told people to leave the centre of the city.

I circled many opened streets and desperately hoped to find my two children. I eventually got caught by the South Vietnamese soldiers, who told me that I had to leave this central part of the city. I decided to ride the bicycle home and found that my two children were already home. They had been found by my oldest son. They were thirsty and hungry from walking a long distance from the school to the centre of the city, where my third daughter had caught sight of her oldest brother walking his bicycle. They told me that they had been unable to get to the van in time to get on. The man had just left, without even waiting for them. They waited for a long time at the school, along with their two friends. Their friends' father came at last on a Vespa to take them home. He advised my children to walk home, since the street was closed and no one could pass the barricades to get to the school. My two children had walked and run, passing through the grass field of the soccer stadium with helicopters hovering above them. They hid in the bush, and then ran until they reached the centre of the city. I washed their dirty and tiny feet while thinking of a way to keep my family safe from the upcoming war, which had shown its dreadful sign at Đà Lạt.

That evening, my wife and I made a decision. We packed some important belongings and all our children into the car and left the city. We planned to take refuge at a Buddhist temple named Trùng Khánh, which belonged to her uncle. Her uncle was a chief monk of the temple. The spacious, beautiful temple was located near Ninh Thuận and Ninh Chử Beach, which belonged to Phan Rang, a small town situated about a three-hour-drive from Đà Lạt. I had often driven my children to visit their granduncle at the temple for their summer vacation. My wife heard and believed that the North Vietnamese soldiers would not attack the temple and that staying with her uncle would be safe.

It turned out that the normally three-hour-drive to Phan Rang was a very slow one. I woke my children up in the middle of the night to leave before dawn. Even so, we could not get to the temple before the sky was dark again. The mountain passes to go down from the plateau were full of walking people who also tried to flee the city. Desperate men and women with young children walked along with slow-moving cars and trucks. The crying of tired, walking children, along with the frustrated voices of men and women, filled the long stretches of the mountain.

Some men swore and threatened to smash my jeep. Some women placed their belongings and their children on the top cover of the jeep's front engine. Some men even hopped onto the railing at the back. My children were so scared and held onto each other inside the green SUV. I told them to close their eyes and try to sleep. My third daughter kept crying quietly throughout the stressful drive. I tried to compose myself while driving slowly among the weary, walking crowds, listening to my wife scolding my third daughter to stop crying.

At dawn, we finally reached the end of the mountain pass and came close to the bridge that connected the highway to Phan Rang. Peoples scattered into more opened fields. The bridges had been damaged by bombing and abandoned belongings were left everywhere along the roads. Some dead bodies were lying on the fields. I decided to drive my car through the creek under the broken bridge. I told my children to raise their feet to avoid getting wet and drove slowly through the stony and shallow creek. My third daughter cried out loud, adding more frustration to everyone.

My children were scared and hungry. My jeep slowly moved past the creek and climbed onto the paved highway. I asked my son to open the side door, and water started to leave the vehicle. We finally had a smooth drive. My third daughter finally stopped crying. My wife and all my children fell asleep for the remainder of the trip. I spotted people, both alive and dead, along the way. I kept on driving and praying. The most fearful factor was to be caught in a gunfight between the North and South Vietnamese soldiers.

I finally reached our destination. The scenery was more peaceful near the road leading to the temple. The Trùng Khánh Buddhist temple had been built in 1924 and reconstructed in 1964. It was situated under the stony mountain and surrounded by hundreds of acres of rice fields. The road leading to the temple was more than a kilometre long, with beautiful palm trees along both sides. While taking my children to the temple for their summer vacations, I loved driving slowly on this road. The wind brought the rich smell of the full rice fields waiting to be harvested. The sound of the palm leaves rustling against each other gave me a sense of peace. The same peaceful feeling eased my fatigue from an intense drive.

I drove to the gate of the temple and received a warm welcome from my wife's uncle, who arranged three rooms in the temple's guest living quarters for us to stay in. My wife and I settled our children into their rooms, and we were served with vegan meals. While the children were sleeping, we went for prayers. We prayed for peace, for the safety of our children, and for being able to return home.

My wife's uncle secretly revealed to us his meditation cave inside the stony mountain behind the temple. While building the temple, he had discovered the cave and built a secret passage connecting his praying quarters to the cave. He said to us that, in a desperate time, this cave would be used for hiding. If the war reached the boundary of the temple, this cave would be the safest place for my family to hide.

My family stayed in the temple for about a month. My oldest daughter was seventeen years old, and my youngest son was three years old. They were well fed and ran freely in the rice fields. They often came back from the rice fields, happily showing me the tiny fish that they had caught in the creek. I told them that the temple forbade killing even a tiny animal. In this peaceful compound, they quickly forgot the war, which was fiercely continuing on in the other parts of the country.

More people came to the temple to find refuge, but the chief monk only accepted a few. I often left the temple and ventured into the city to keep in touch with what was going on. I found that many people gathered at the port every day, waiting for the American ship to come to transport them to Saigon or even to an island near America. I often wondered if I should put my entire family on that American ship. Away from the temple was the full presence of war. Before I left the temple, my third daughter always worried and asked me to make sure that I would come back. I lied to her that

I would only go to buy her favorite baguette. Before I got to the port to see more people board the ship and leave the city, I always made sure to buy the baguette first. She and her brother often played near the gate to wait for me. They yelled happily, greeting me each time I came back with the baguette. Their innocence in this peaceful temple hindered my decision of putting my family to this risky and unsure trip. I was not sure if all the news I heard from the people who gathered at the port were true.

The war slowly revealed itself at the temple gate. That day, the helicopters were hovering atop the temple. More South Vietnamese soldiers were deployed, and gunfights with the North Communist soldiers happened in the rice fields. My wife and I took our children and hid in the secret cave. On the way to the cave, bullets were flying over our heads. We cuddled each other in the cave, hearing the sound of the bullets breaking the stones on top of the cave into pieces. My six young children were crying, but my three older children were calm. I realized that it was not the first time that my three older children had experienced this. Back in 1970, when my young family lived in Quảng Đức, we had hidden in the family's underground cave when facing bombings and gunfights.

People broke the temple gate to find refuge. Dead bodies were found in the rice fields. Finally, the North Communist soldiers came to the temple and demanded to talk to the chief monk. They asked the temple to provide them with cooked rice. Every day, a group of North Vietnamese soldiers arrived and politely ate their portion of rice, which had been placed on the main hall steps. The different groups came in the morning and the afternoon, just to eat the rice. They only asked for rice and salt. They said nothing but acted politely to everyone. My children helped the monks to cook the rice for them every day. They often asked me why North Vietnamese soldiers only ate rice with salt. I made up an answer for my children, saying that the North Vietnamese soldiers were vegans.

People started to leave the temple, and the dead bodies were cleared from the rice fields. The monks continued with their rituals every day. The North Vietnamese soldiers stopped coming to eat rice. On April 30, 1975, the news was broadcast by radio that the war was over. The North Communist soldiers had completely taken over South Vietnam. My wife announced to my children that peace had finally arrived in Vietnam. The last American had left Vietnam, and there would be no more fighting between the North and the South. The war had officially ended.

We left the temple and drove home. Our home was still in great shape. For the next few years, my wealth started to be confiscated. It started with the currency exchange. All families and citizens had to turn in all old currency and be started anew with a small amount of North Vietnamese currency. Those who worked for the American and the South Vietnamese officials were sent to prisons for political reform.

My children had to fill out papers at school to list their family background. Families listed in a certain category were forced away from their homes to go to an economic-reform area. In the neighborhood, a family refused to leave, and all the family members committed suicide. Many families came back from the economic-reformed land and lived on the street, since they had lost their homes. The pharmacy my wife and I owned was confiscated, along with the family's green SUV. The top communist policemen came to my home in Đà Lạt and confiscated the telephone, the typewriter, the fridge, and the television.

My wife sewed gold ingots into the lining of the clothes, and made my children wear them without knowing it. My wife and I gathered rare medicines and hid them in between the roof and under the mattress, where my youngest daughter slept. They came into my home, trying to find my gold, but I baited them with obvious things, which they busily took away. They were somewhat satisfied with the telephone, the typewriter, the fridge, and the television without finding my gold ingots. The hidden gold and rare medicines kept my family surviving for years, until the first planned escape in 1981.

My children were all at home at the time the policemen carried out the confiscation. They were terrified and sitting all together on one bed, trying to keep the family dog quiet. Throughout the ordeal, I tried to remain calm, but my blood was boiling from the inside. My wife thought my anger would bust open my veins at any time. I thought that, as soon as they demanded to search my children, I would grab their guns and fight back. However, they were not violent. They just carefully examined things and carried them out of the house. Before they left, I noticed that one policeman kept looking at the family dog.

The next day, I was summoned to the central police station, and the policeman told me that they wanted my family dog. I found out that my next-door neighbour was also summoned and asked to turn in their dog as well. My neighbour's home was not being searched, and none of his assets were confiscated. It happened that they had let their pet dog out in the front yard while the policemen were at my house. The policeman had noticed it.

I came home not knowing what to tell my children. Strangely, the children told me that the dogs refused to play with them. Both dogs were making sad sounds and kept to themselves in the corners of the house. Surprised, I wondered how the dogs knew.

The policemen came to the house faster than I could inform my children. In front of all the children, they tied the dogs, one by one, on the leash. The children cried. The dogs wailed. Tears were running from the children's eyes and from the dogs' as well. The policemen decided to tie the mouths of the animals. The animals knew the end of their lives had arrived. They refused to leave. They spread their legs to fight being pulled. Helplessly, they were dragged away. Their paws made shrieking sounds and left long stretches of lines on the cement. I told all the children to go inside the house. They did not listen but went running after the animals. When they could not hold on to the animals, they screamed. Tears also came from my eyes. The day before, they had lost their television and their fridge, and had not shed a tear.

My children and my next-door neighbour's children cried for their pet dogs for months. They knew what had really happened to the animals after they were taken away by the policemen. I could not comfort my children. I often told my children that, when the animals died, they would be reincarnated into humans. According to Buddhist belief, it was a good thing for an animal to die. However, this theory did not help my children with their pain from losing their pet in such a dramatic way.

In these turbulent times, vulnerabilities were everywhere. Humans and animals suffered. Death was a few centimeters from life. Was there real peace, as had been declared on April 30, 1975?

THE BEST GIFT

16

1971 - 1983
ĐÀ LẠT

ĐÀ LẠT IS A PLATEAU SITUATED NOT FAR from Quảng Đức, and somehow this peaceful location was protected from the war. I bought a house near Linh Sơn temple and settled my family in. The years of 1971 to 1975 were the best years of our lives. I had more free time for my children. I arranged for my three oldest children to enroll in the best school. I registered my third daughter and my third son to learn in a prestigious French School. I opened a pharmacy store for my wife to run, and she also practiced as an on-call nurse. I often took business trips to bigger cities to buy medications for our store. Our life was peaceful on this plateau. My family grew bigger with two more sons and one more daughter. My ten living children were my true wealth. They were my source of energy and passion. Each of them brought happiness to me, specially and uniquely. They were my immense treasure of bliss.

I often took my children to the temple to expose them to

the religion and to appreciate the simple but precious peaceful life. The temple was so near to our home and became more like a playground for my children. They often took the shortcut through the temple ground. My two younger sister families followed me to move away from Huế, our hometown, to build their lives in Đà Lạt. Their houses were not far from where my family lived. My extended family also grew. I often arranged family vacations and took my children, my nieces, and my nephews back to Huế to visit my mother, who lived with my younger brother's family. We celebrated every Lunar New Year in harmony, hearing the temple bell echoing for three consecutive days. The temple also raised turtles and built their habitat inside the temple compound. Their shells were engraved with Buddhist characters to represent harmony and peace.

I taught my children to respect the living and the dead. Two years after I left Quảng Đức, I came back to this still-war infested land. I came back to exhume the bodies of my two children who had died from an illness. Their remains were sealed in clay pots and hidden in black luggage. The day I came back from the trip, my second son greeted me at the door. My children often got gifts from me when I came back from a long trip. They were excited to open the luggage to find their gifts. My son was so curious that I did not allow him to bring the black luggage inside the house. I did not tell him what was in it.

I had already arranged for my two dead children's remains to be buried near their relatives. According to religious belief, dead bodies were forbidden to enter a house. Therefore, I had to leave the black luggage outside and asked my sons to guard it until it was brought to the Linh Sơn temple, from which they could be buried in the Mã Thánh cemetery, which was only a few kilometres away from my home.

My second son remembered this event. He probably guessed what was inside the mysterious black luggage. I never explained to him what I was doing. However, he learned from what I did. At that moment, I ignited his curiosity by telling him just to guard the luggage but not touch it. He knew that the dead had to be respected and needed to be near their living relatives.

I never expected the same thing would happen to me. Twelve years later, I was dead. It was a lonely death. My body was exhumed from Côn Sơn Island and transported to Đà Lạt. I was buried at Du Sinh cemetery without my children. My grave was halfway around the earth from my living children. Forty-two years after I reburied my dead children in Đà Lạt, my second and fifth sons came back from America to bring me nearer to them. They also placed my cremated ash in a small travel bag and brought me onto a plane, which flew from Vietnam to America.

17

MY MOTHER

I WAS MY MOTHER'S FAVOURITE CHILD. SHE WAS proud that
I was a filial son to her and a generous brother to all family
members. She told me that I'd received all the blessings from
the family ancestors. She often repeated herself, telling me
that I was born in the year of the tiger and bore its spirit.
I got all the courage to travel far from my hometown to
build a better life for my family. From that, I could help my
extended family to prosper. During my time in Quảng Đức,
I often visited my mother and brought her gifts. I used part
of my wealth to build for her a bigger house with a better
room to light more incenses to thank the ancestors.

In her old age and near the end of her life, she stayed
with my younger brother's family. My mother lived until
she was ninety-six years old. She died in 1989, four years
after my death. My regular visits to my mother stopped in
1985. My younger brother kept my death a secret from my
mother. He thought that, if she knew about my tragic death,
sorrow would negatively affect her health. She was told that

I had reunited with my children who lived in Canada. She questioned my younger brother as to why she never got any letters from me. Hearing no words from me was odd. It was completely out of my character. Her memory was not as sharp with old age. However, when she remembered and missed me, she cried and kept asking my brother to let her know where I was.

A week before she passed away, she asked my younger brother to let her stay in the house that I built for her. She packed a few belongings and left for her house. She lit incense and prayed to hear from me. That evening, while my mother was sleeping, I visited her. I was only a ghost. I had come to realize that no one could see me. Perhaps, though, they could sense my presence as a spirit. My desire to be with my love ones was so strong and severe enough to leave an effect on their feelings or even to trigger their sixth sense. As a ghost, I stood beside my mother's bed watching her, and I wanted to hug her. I wanted to say how sorry I was that I had left this world before her. She suddenly opened her eyes. At that moment, I felt our eyes meet each other's. She could see me.

The next morning, my younger brother came to visit her. My mother cried and scolded my younger brother for hiding the fact that I was dead. She said that she could not understand what had made me go into the ocean and die with my youngest daughter. Upon hearing that, my younger brother was so scared. Somehow, she knew that I had died with my youngest daughter during the horrendous escape. He lit more incense and prayed for the ancestors to soothe my spirit.

Three days later, my mother peacefully passed away. She could see me. She joined me in death. She smiled and hugged me. She knew that I had defied my death. She understood that I had left so much undone on earth and wanted to remain between life and death. My soul had not been able to find peace. My spirit maintained its unrested state and could not break free of the living. Again, I remained as a ghost wandering on earth. The moment after her death, my mother had to leave. I felt her embrace for the last time before her spirit rose to Heaven.

18

MY CHILDREN

THE SAME YEAR OF MY MOTHER'S DEATH, MY wife and my two youngest sons were able to leave Vietnam for Canada. Their sponsorship was finally approved by the communist government and accepted by the Canadian delegation to leave the country. The original paper, which was sent in 1984, included my name and my youngest daughter's name. Again, my wife's younger brother helped her. He bribed the high-ranking officials to clear the family's sin and tainted record. My name and my youngest daughter's name were erased from the sponsorship paper.

My spirit followed my wife and my two youngest sons. They arrived in Canada in June of 1989. My wife, a widow, was only fifty-four years old. Over the years, my surviving children grieved my death and their youngest sister's death in agony. They could never find the solution for their question: Why could I not wait until I could leave the country legally? What had made me try the third attempt, while I was already holding the sponsorship paper? This unanswered question made my death and my youngest daughter's death even harder for them to accept.

However, they did not let hardship and grief prevent them from achieving their goals. My children worked hard to earn enough money to support themselves and managed to continue their education. They lived frugally to be able to send money back to Vietnam to help their mother, sister, and younger brothers. My oldest daughter's family was also sponsored to migrate, and joined them in Canada a few years later. My family was finally reunited.

Ironically, I could only be with my children as a ghost. I longed to be able to embrace each of my children in my arms. My youngest son was only fifteen years old. From teenagers to adults, they all needed guidance and support. I wanted to hear them complain to me about all the hardship that they had been through, from their escape to the time they spent in the refugee camp in Indonesia. I wished I could tell them how sorry I was that I'd had to die before I could complete my responsibilities to them as a father. I wished to tell them that I was even more empathetic when I could not be there for them, in every moment of their happiness and their sorrows.

I had left my children too soon. In their fatherless remaining lives, I'd left my life for them to continue. I left what I had taught them to realize that they had to put all that they had learned from me into practice. One important lesson I had taught my children was the value of education. My children worked hard to support themselves and managed to continue with their education. They became responsible citizens in their new country.

Back in Đà Lạt, during a peaceful time, I'd installed a blackboard on the wall in the room next to the kitchen. I often wrote a list of chores for them to complete throughout the day on that board. Studying was the priority during evening time, before any bedtime games or stories. Some days, I wrote math problems on the blackboard, riddles for them to challenge among brothers and sisters. During their summer vacation, I taught them the trades in drawing, using the electric pen to burn the wood board and to create beautiful pictures. They were also taught how to sew winter hats using animal furs.

My children maintained the family tradition and were embedded in well-taught disciplines. They all became very successful in their education, in their careers, and at the same time, very devoted, loving, and responsible parents. Five of my sons followed their engineering careers and business ventures, and moved to America.

My spirit stayed with my beloved children who settled in both Canada and America. For more than thirty years of living in new countries, they have lived their lives for me.

Each of my sons carried in them a part of my character. My oldest son is like a willow—a willow tree, which bends easily but is almost unbreakable. My second son, who was born in the year of the tiger, always carried a sense of humor like me, but with wise and deep thoughts. My third son, who spent two years of his youth on the family-built boat, carried out my business ambition in this new land. He continued with my legacy and became a successful businessman. He left Canada after completing his first engineering degree and ventured to America. He found a land where he could practice his business ambition. The similarity was that I had left Huế and moved to Quảng Đức to start my business. He became the pillar of the extended family and brought his brothers to America to join him.

My fourth son lived a life that I did not have. He lived a carefree but balanced life, dedicated to his wife and his career. My fifth son, who survived the escape in 1985, was extremely smart, detail-oriented, and devoted. My sixth son, who also survived the fatal escape, was diligent and enduring. All my children carried in them many hidden talents in arts and music. Their talents bloomed, with high moral, meaningful, and successful lives that they built on.

My flesh was present in my children. My blood flowed in my children. Their intelligence surpassed their father. Each of my children lived and reflected a unique part of a life that I had lived and had also missed.

I wanted to tell my children that I left them too soon. My physical presence as a father to them was short, but my spirit as a father to them was eternal. My love for them remained a lifetime and lived on in many generations to come.

19

MY WIFE
THE LOVE OF MY LIFE

I MET MY WIFE FOR THE FIRST TIME in 1956, when she boarded the bus from Đà Lạt to Mũi Né, Bình Thuận. She was a nursing student and in her work term at the main hospital of Đà Lạt. Her hometown was Mũi Né, which was a fishing town located by the ocean closer to the south of Vietnam. I was thirty years old and in my last year at the military school in Đà Lạt. I was allowed a short leave to visit my mother at my hometown of Huế. Fate had arranged for us to have leave at the same time and also to board the same bus. The bus would stop at Phan Thiết, and from there it would continue its journey to Huế. Phan Thiết was a city near Mũi Né. While boarding the bus, I was asked by the bus driver to help with the passengers' luggage. I was assigned to help a group, and among the passengers was a beautiful and smart young nursing student.

She asked me gently to be careful while handling her luggage, since it contained fragile medical equipment. Along with that, she gave me a warm smile. At that moment, the world of love unveiled its mystery to me. It never occurred to me that I would get married in this war. I was already thirty years old and was considered too old to be married. I was also in military school and preparing to be assigned to war zones. Love came to my life as a surprise and worked mysteriously with its miracles, one by one.

I fell in love with the lovely young nursing student at first sight. Months after that, I would skip classes and borrow my superior's jeep to pick her up after her shifts at the hospital. Đà Lạt held a romantic reason for me to bring my family back there to live in 1971. Our love started on that peaceful plateau, grew, and blossomed into marriage in 1957.

Our first home was in Huế, my hometown. My father gave us a piece of land to build our first home. Before I graduated, I switched to office training in military school and studied architecture. In moving back to Huế, my wife was practicing as an on-call nurse while caring for our young family. After four years in Huế, I moved to Quảng Đức so that I could put my architecture training into practice.

It was twenty-nine years from the day I met and fell in love with my wife to the day of my death. I left her alone on this earth while she was only fifty-one years old, a widow with nine children, ranging from twenty-eight to thirteen years old. I left my wife another twenty-six years of loneliness and sorrows. Among those twenty-six years, there were many years of grief, tormented by my death.

"My dear wife, the love of my life, I want to tell you that you grieved for me and our daughter's death for so long. Your grief measured as long as your remaining lifetime. I saw it in your eyes every time you looked, in your walk every time you took a step. Your eyes hold hidden tears, and your clothes dripped with the burden of sadness. I longed for you to be able to hear my voice, to tell you how regretful I was to leave you with the immense sorrow and unhappiness, if my words could give you any comfort or relief. Fate cruelly cut our love short. Instead of a lifetime together, you lived your remaining life with an aching soul."

My wife remained a widow for the rest of her life. She became very ill when she turned seventy-four. My third son took her to America to live close to her sons, and she was placed in the best medical care. When my third daughter stayed with her in the hospital, she told my daughter that she was so happy to see me so clearly and so often in her dreams. It was part of her happiness being able to have a good night's sleep and dream about me—about our life together. She said that she dreamt of cooking outside, and then the rain suddenly came. She saw me helping her bring the small stove inside. The image was so vivid that she thought she saw me for real.

Coincidently, our first home had an outdoor kitchen. She also dreamt that we went grocery shopping together at a flea market. The rain came again then, and we held each other's hands and ran to find shelter. When we went under a big umbrella to avoid the rain, she looked up, and I was gone. She interpreted the dream to my daughter, saying that she was glad that her father, me, did not have to see her suffering from illness in her old age.

When we fell in love, she asked me if I would still fall in love with her when she was no longer young and beautiful.

Would Heaven take both of us from the earth at the same time to spare us from missing each other?

"My dearest wife, my love for you was eternal. I loved you in life and also in death, from this life, and into our next life. Our love bloomed, grew, and lived on in our beautiful children. When I died, I could not step through the door of Heaven. I wanted to be with you, to drift beside you as a ghost, to continue loving you as a ghost. I figured I would also be lonely if I stayed in Heaven while you remained on this earth. I realized that I could not bear to see you grieving for me in loneliness. I wanted to continue our responsibilities to our children. My conscience tormented me with the fact of leaving you to take care of our children on your own. I never wanted to accept that our love life was divided and interrupted by death. I waited for you, forever, in living and in death. I waited for you as a ghost, so that when you were about to enter the door of Heaven, I would be there for you. We would be able to see each other again. We would be able to hold our hands and entered the door of Heaven together."

20

TO MY DAUGHTER
HOÀNG THỊ DIỆU PHƯƠNG
THE BEST GIFT TO GIVE TO THE DEAD

EACH OF MY CHILDREN GRIEVED FOR MY DEATH and their sister's death at a different level. It did not matter how busy their daily lives were, the grief would creep its way in at any time. My children were young when I died. They grew up missing a huge part of the parents' love. They became parents themselves, but had not yet fully experienced the love of their parents. There was always a crack or a hole which could not be filled.

My third daughter grieved deeply, and over thirty years, she still never could accept the deaths of her father and her youngest sister. Perhaps, because she had only heard about the death, she denied it. She could not attend my first or second funerals. The reality was not there yet for her to accept my death. She could hardly let her grief go. Perhaps, my spirit, remaining as a ghost, was so strong that she felt me and longed to be able to see me.

I longed to tell my daughter that I was sorry I had left this world so soon. I left leaving many lessons untaught, many questions unanswered, many pieces of advice not yet spoken, and many wounds unhealed.

My third daughter and her family came back to Vietnam in 2008. She only had a vague idea of where my grave was located at Du Sinh Cemetery. However, among hundreds and thousands of clustering graves, she was able to find mine. She wanted to prove that my presence as a ghost and living among my children was real. She believed that my spirit guided her to the exact location of my grave. She lit incense for me and shed tears that she had held in for so many years. On that hill, in the gentle wind, I wished I could whisper to her that the best gift she could give to the dead was to forget. If she could not practice letting go, then "to forget" was the best medicine to cure her immense sorrow.

The Best Gift.

My hands last trembled in the dark, cruel wave
Sinking my lifeless body, yet I still felt I could fly
Had night passed? Why did morning come so fast?
Darkness came, but light chased it away
I closed my eyes, but I could only see the bright light
Death arriving and life departing
Entering Heaven yet defying
Farewell, my loved ones
Forgive me for leaving you all too soon
Forget me please... It is your best gift
Given to the living and to the dead.

21

2015
MY THIRD FUNERAL

MY WIFE PASSED AWAY IN THE LATE SUMMER of 2010. She was buried in Orange County, California. In April 2015, twenty-nine years after I was buried for the second time at Du Sinh Cemetery, my second son and my fifth son took a trip to Vietnam. All brothers and sisters agreed to the suggestion of my third daughter, that my remains should be buried near the living relatives.

On that sunny day in Đà Lạt, my sons, my relatives, a monk, and the cemetery worker team arrived at my grave. They lit incense on my grave for the last time. The month chanted Buddhist scriptures and prayed. After that, the cemetery workers took turns to dig. They kept my tombstone intact and dug narrowly down. Unlike searching and digging to find my body in Côn Sơn Island, they knew exactly what to do, and the heavy rain did not come.

They finally reached my coffin and began to raise it. Everything was still intact. They opened my coffin and my bones were exposed to the air for the third and final time. My bones had stayed healthy and completely preserved, despite being underneath that ground for twenty-nine years. The red cloth, which was used to wrap my bones, retained its color and its shape. My sons wanted to feel me for the last time. No words could express their deep emotion. Their trembling hands reached into my opened coffin, and they wept. I felt drops of their tears on my bones. They lovingly embraced me with the flesh of their warm hands.

They also exhumed the remains of their brother and their sister, and put them all in the same coffin. From there, the remains were transferred to a cremation centre. They then put my remains in a sealed clay urn, and their brother and sister in another one. My two sons carefully put the clay urns in their travel bag and disguised them. They were able to board a taxi and plane to Saigon without anyone knowing that they were travelling with the dead.

Twenty-nine years ago, my wife and my nephew-in-law also hid my remains in their travel bag. When my sons arrived at Saigon, they had to apply for the official paper-work for me to leave Vietnam. They obtained the permit. At the Saigon airport, before boarding the plane, the communist official put a stamp on my paper to allow me to leave Vietnam.

My urn of ashes left Vietnam and went on the plane to legally enter America in 2015. It took thirty years after my death for my remains to rest close to my loved ones. All my living children united together and gave me another grand funeral. All my children took turns to respectfully place their hands on the clay urn that contained my ashes. They all embraced me. It was a precious and once-in-a-lifetime moment that they had been able to achieve for themselves and for me. They fulfilled my wish to be able to embrace them again. They fulfilled my wish to be able to unite with them in America. I was buried together with my wife. I joined her in death and was able to be with her in the same grave.

22

LETTING GO

MY SOUL WANDERED AIMLESSLY AMONG THE LIVING ON this earth for thirty years after that fatal day in the ocean.

I had lived it all. From the moment I was born in a war-torn country until I breathed my last breath in the Pacific Ocean of a country which had found its peace.

I had seen it all. From the moment I left my children fatherless, young, innocent, and helpless, to the moment they matured, wise and successful.

I had felt it all. From the moment my family was divided, and my children began to painfully grieve my death, to the moment my family was reunited and my children finally let me go.

I had experienced it all. From the moment I fell in love with my wife ... joy, happiness, sorrow, and suffering, until we could only see each other in our dreams and be joined together as ashes.

I had learned it all. From the moment my spirit left my lifeless body, denying and defying until I needed to rest my weary soul.

God appeared before me again. God reopened the door for me. God held my hands and led me through the door of Heaven.

AUTHOR'S NOTE

I USED TO HATE THE OCEAN. I REFUSED any trips that took me near the ocean. I refrained from seeing its sign printed in the poster. I avoided watching any movie with the ocean, ships, or boats tied with its theme. The ocean had sunk my heart in deep sorrow and filled it with a painful memory of my father and my sister's deaths. Its waves swallowed my father's last breath. Its salty water dissolved my sister's flesh. Somewhere in the darkness of its abyss, my father's last words echoed and my sister's bones scattered.

Year after year, from adolescence to adulthood, my hatred of the ocean minimized its strength. From single life to married life, I reminded myself that I needed to forgive the ocean, so that I could face its sight. My children loved vacations, swimming in the warm ocean and playing with its soft white sands. Finally, the sound of the ocean waves mixed with my children's laughter and created a tranquil vibration, which travelled through my heart and eased its wounds.

Dearest Father,

You have taught me that many ships set sail into the vast seas. They faced the same waves and the same winds created by the atmospheric pressure and the ocean's depth. However, one ship could depart its dock and travel to the west or to the east; another ship could come back to the port from the north or from the south. Its direction was not set by the winds or the waves but by human predetermination. Your teachings concluded that, like those ships sailing into the sea, and despite how cruel fate could be, I could control my destiny. I realize that life threw its tribulation to articulate your ingenuity, your courage, and your self-sacrifice.

Dear God,

In my next life, please let me be my father's daughter again.

THE END

ACKNOWLEDGEMENTS

I AM IMMENSELY GRATEFUL TO MY PARENTS. YOU gave me life. You instilled in me a solid sense of discipline and responsibility. Your hardship, struggle, success, and enduring love to raise ten children inspired me and shaped my inner strength.

I am grateful to Judy and John Smith, who founded the Hamilton Mountain Fund to help Vietnamese Boat People. Your decision gave us a country and our futures.

My deepest gratitude and forever love to my beloved children: Helen Diệu Thương Trần, Christie Hoàng Thương Trần, and Charlotte Emily Như Thương Trần. You all are my greatest accomplishment, my dream, my life, and my everything. Your curiosity and persistent questions about your roots encouraged me to write this book. From the start to the end, this writing journey has healed me from prolonged grieving and inner suffering.

I am grateful to my grandchildren: Cora and Oliver. You fill my life with joy and complete it with more never-ending love.

I am grateful to my brothers and sisters.

To my oldest sister, Hoàng Thị Mỹ Phương, for your diligence of maintaining family pictures and memorabilia.

To my oldest brother, Hoàng Trọng Phiên, for your gentleness and your story of the monkey.

To my older sister, Hoàng Thị Hằng Phương, for your practical mind and many delicious meals.

To my younger brother Hoàng Trọng Phi, for your optimistic views and your cheerfulness.

To my younger brother Hoàng Trọng Phấn, for your patience and your empathy.

To my older brother Hoàng Trọng Phán, for your wittiness and your decisive mind.

To my younger brother Hoàng Trọng Phổ, for your intelligence and meticulousness. Together with our older brother Hoàng Trọng Phán, you went back to Vietnam in April of 2015 and brought our father to America. You fulfilled his deepest wish.

And especially to my older brother Hoàng Trọng Phú, for your compassion, wisdom, and generosity. You are the third son, who together with Uncle Hoàng Thế Thái, navigated the boat our father built, and successfully and safely brought us to Indonesia, where our new life began. You are an important part of this book. I am thankful for your compliments and your enthusiasm in reading the manuscript from its fragile beginning to its imperfect ending. You often consoled me, and reminded me to publish this book. I am forever grateful to you.

I am grateful to Uncle Hoàng Thế Thái, for your courage and your generous compliments to my imperfect guitar skills, while playing the chords along with my singing of the songs "Mùa Thu Lá Bay" and "Bay Đi Cánh Chim Biển," during the time at the refugee camp, where waiting to settle in a third country seemed an eternity.

I am grateful to all sisters-in-law, brothers-in-law, son-in-law, nieces-in-law and nephews-in-law for your love to the Hoàng and the Trần. You completed our extended family.

I am grateful to my nieces and nephews: Andy, Vicky, Timothy, Peter, Joshua, Jacqueline, Tammy, Timmy, Lily, Andrew, Amy-Anna, Ethan, Allison, Kim, Bill, and Will. You are the next generation of the Hoàng. I compliment all of you for your inner beauty, your talents, your humbleness, and your appreciation of your roots.

I am grateful to all my teachers and professors, who taught me and gave me knowledge.

I am grateful to my secret best friend. You are an important part of my life. You made my past. You taught me that life is not all about discipline and responsibility. Life also consists of excitement, exuberance and bewilderment.

I am thankful for mathematics. You defined my living and my career. Your no-nonsense approach and your nature of right or wrong pull me back into focus whenever my mind is scattered with numerous tangling and wondering thoughts.

I am also appreciative to the FriesenPress teams who assisted me in turning this manuscript into a book. This book would not be possible without all of you.

ABOUT THE AUTHOR

A math professor at Niagara College, located in Welland, Ontario, Jolie P. Hoang escaped Vietnam in 1983, two years before her father and youngest sister perished in their attempt to escape to freedom. Their deaths affected her deeply, and she only managed to find inner peace upon the completion of this book, which came very much from the heart. She hopes that the next generations of her family will be inspired by his sacrifice, and with this volume, learn more about their roots.

Jolie lives with her daughters in Fonthill, Ontario.

CPSIA information can be obtained
at www.ICGtesting.com
Printed in the USA
LVHW050433180920
666285LV00020B/1236